better together*

*This book is best read together, grownup and kid.

a
kids
book
about

a kids book about BEING INCLUSIVE

by Ashton Mota & Rebekah Bruesehoff
in partnership with *The GenderCool Project*

A Kids Co.
Editor Denise Morales Soto
Designers Rick DeLucco & Duke Stebbins
Creative Director Rick DeLucco
Studio Manager Kenya Feldes
Sales Director Melanie Wilkins
Head of Books Jennifer Goldstein
CEO and Founder Jelani Memory

DK
Editor Emma Roberts
Senior Production Editor Jennifer Murray
Senior Production Controller Louise Minihane
Senior Acquisitions Editor Katy Flint
Acquisitions Project Editor Sara Forster
Managing Art Editor Vicky Short
Publishing Director Mark Searle

This American Edition, 2024
Published in the United States by DK Publishing
1745 Broadway, 20th Floor, New York, NY 10019

DK, a Division of Penguin Random House LLC

23 24 25 26 27 10 9 8 7 6 5 4 3 2 1
001-339156-April/2024

Published in Great Britain by Dorling Kindersley Limited.

A catalog record for this book is available from the Library of Congress.
ISBN: 978-0-7440-9472-5

Printed and bound in China

www.dk.com

akidsco.com

This book was made with Forest Stewardship Council™ certified paper – one small step in DK's commitment to a sustainable future.
Learn more at www.dk.com/uk/information/sustainability

To every kiddo out there who is living
the life they were always meant to live,
and to the grownups who believe in them.

To all our GenderCool Champion friends
whose voices helped make this book a reality.
We are changing the world: Alex, Chazzie,
Daniel, Eve, Gia, Greyson, Hunter, Jonathan, Kai,
Landon, Lia, Max, Rose, Sivan, Stella, and Tru.

Intro
for grownups

This is a book about the choices we make as human beings to help those around us be seen and feel valued. Being inclusive is one of the most satisfying, healthy, and positive behaviors we can teach ourselves and the kids in our lives. It also helps us see the world around us in the clearest possible way. Inclusion starts with opening ourselves up to people who aren't like us, whether that be differences in gender, race, ethnicity, religion, ability—the list is endless! If we're serious about creating a world where everyone feels welcomed, we need to start with inclusion.

So, let's breathe life into this beautiful behavior. Let's talk about real examples of being inclusive. Let's learn from 2 remarkable young people who are here to help through the power of their stories.

Welcome! We're so glad you're here.

—The GenderCool Team

Hi everyone! I'm **Rebekah**.

My pronouns are she/her
and I love to laugh!

Rebekah

And my name is **Ashton**!

I use he/him pronouns
and I love spending time
with my friends and family!

Ashton

Ashton and I met through **The GenderCool Project**, and now we are really great friends.

Rebekah

We want to explore
what being inclusive
means and would love
for you to join us.

What do you think?

If that sounds fun to you,
just turn the page!

Have you ever heard
the word **inclusion**?

How about **inclusive**?

Maybe you've heard these words from a teacher or another grownup but didn't know what they mean.

Well, **inclusion** is kind of like sharing...

BUT B

GGER.

It's a choice we make
every day to accept people
and believe they're awesome
for being exactly who they are!

Being inclusive means celebrating everyone in all their uniqueness and making sure nobody feels left out!

Rebekah

Growing up, I didn't really feel included.

I always felt like I didn't fit in or didn't belong. At the time, I wasn't quite sure why until I found the word to describe who I am...That word for me is **transgender**.

Ashton

Even though my friends and family sometimes didn't quite understand the way I felt, they always showed they cared, reminded me they loved me, and wanted the best for me.

That made me super happy!

Ashton

I’m transgender too!

When I was born,
everyone thought I was a boy,
but I always knew I was a girl.

My family loved and
supported me, which allowed
me to do the things I love,
like reading and playing
in the woods.

Rebekah

Being transgender
isn't a choice.

It's who we are.

But being inclusive?
Yeah, that's a choice!

Rebekah

Since our families were able
to show us what it was like
to be inclusive, it became
really easy for us to do
the same.

Being inclusive isn't
about making all our
differences the same.

It's about welcoming
everyone as they are.

Look! We'll show you.

Have you ever
gone to class late?

It can be a little
awkward, right?

You're nervous and kind of embarrassed because everyone is already there, and now they're all staring at you, and you feel kind of frozen.

But if you look around
and see someone smiling
at you—it doesn't seem
all that bad anymore.

You feel welcome,
and like you aren't
bothering anyone
by being late.

Giving a little wave or just having a smile on your face can be inclusive!

It doesn't even matter if you don't know someone that well!

Just say hi.

Sometimes that's all it takes for someone to feel less alone.

But maybe the person
who came into class late
didn’t only feel excluded
because they were late.

I know I've had that same feeling, even when I was right on time.

I felt out of place when I was the only transgender kid in the class. It felt like no one would understand, and I was nervous.

Rebekah

Now that I think
about it, me too.

Sometimes at school,
I look around and I don't
see too many people that
look like me or my family.
It kind of makes me feel
like the star of the show...

but not in a good way.

Ashton

A lot of times, people can
feel excluded because of
their skin color, or their religion,
their gender, the way they dress,
if they have a disability,
what language they speak—
and for so many other reasons.

Even though we're all
different from one another, we
all want to be part of the group.

We all want to feel included.

But the cool thing is,
differences make us special.
And they don't have to be BIG.

Little differences are just as important!

Ashton

Rebekah

The fact that we're different brings us closer together, because we always have something new to talk about and share.

If we all loved the same things...

that would be boring!

Hey, Rebekah,
didn't you just move?

Ashton

Yeah!

This year, I'm the new kid at school.

Rebekah

Honestly, it was scary to walk into school on the first day because I wasn't sure I would make any friends. I didn't want to be left out either.

But when someone came over and asked me what my name was, I felt better getting to know someone else! It turned out we have the same birthday!

Rebekah

Have you ever moved, Ashton?

Rebekah

Well, no, but every year at my school we have tons of new kids, and this year I made a really cool friend!

One day at lunch,
I was eating with them
and when they opened up
their lunch box, I noticed
that they'd brought food
I had never seen before.

Ashton

I was kind of nervous because I didn't want to ask what it was and hurt their feelings, but it looked so good that I had to do it.

They didn't mind at all!

They were actually excited I was interested. They even let me try some, and it was delicious!

Ashton

That's awesome!

Rebekah

You see?

It's about making
a genuine effort to reach
out to someone, learn,
and accept them
for who they are.

Rebekah

Another big part of being
inclusive is noticing
who isn't there.

Who's being left out?

You have to choose
to see who’s left out,
then choose to include
them so they feel like they
are a part of things.

Here’s an example:

imagine you and your friends are all playing tag.

Everyone is running around and laughing, having a great time.

You don’t want to stop playing, but then you notice someone sitting alone.

You could go over to them and
ask if they want to play too.

THAT'S BEING
INCLU

And now you have a **new friend**!

The truth is...

It was really fun!

But do you want to hear something really cool?

The journey isn't over. It keeps going.

Ashton

That's right! Go out there and discover all the **BILLIONS** of ways you can be more inclusive in your life!

Rebekah

So, take action.
Choose to be inclusive.

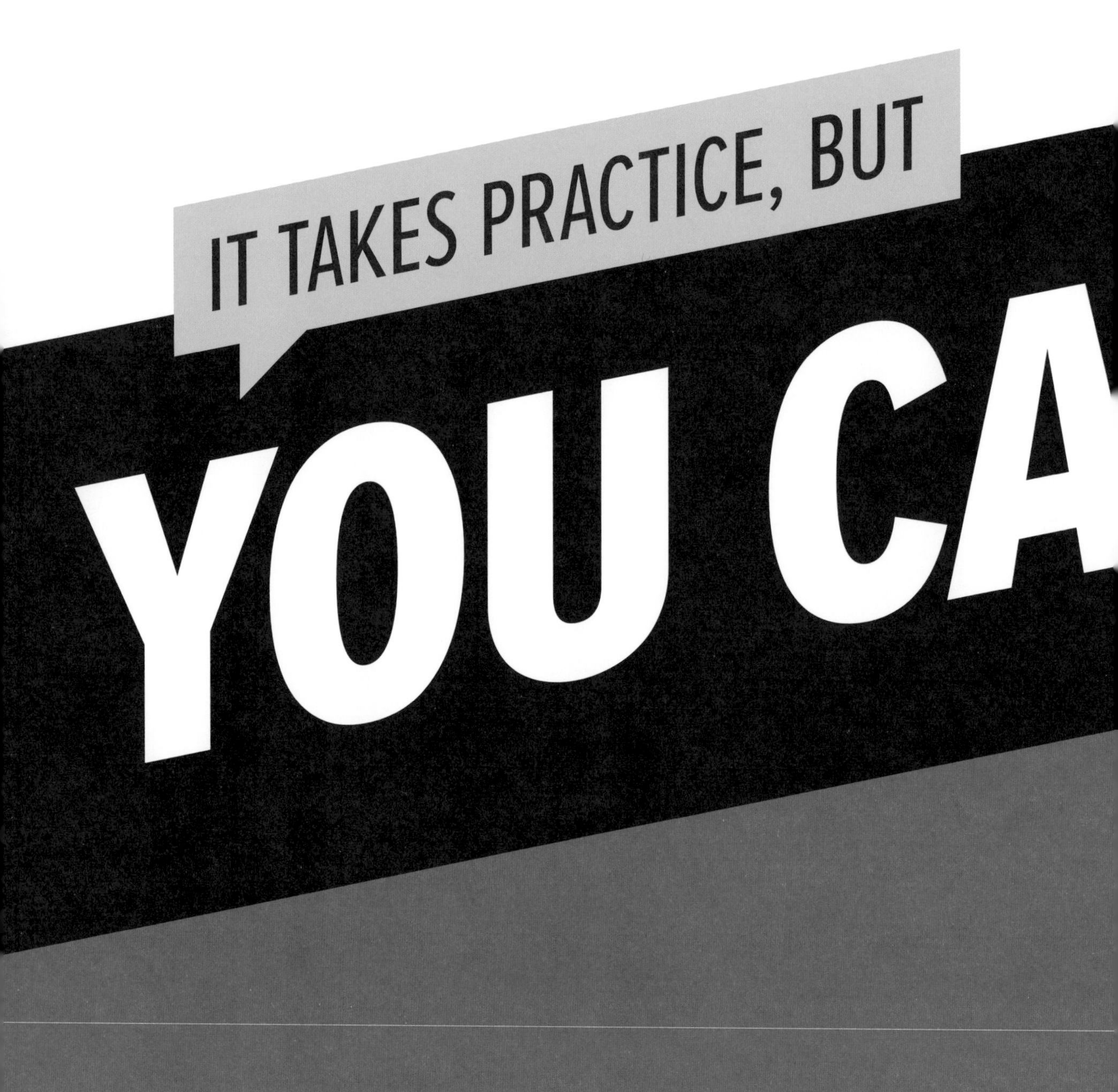

N DO IT!

Continue your journey
of being more inclusive
every day.

Because when we
are inclusive, we help
others **THRIVE**!

Outro
for grownups

It doesn't matter where you live, what you look like, how old you are, or how much money you have—everyone has the power to be inclusive. It starts with caring about helping people feel welcomed, valued, and good about themselves.

Here's where it gets interesting: you have to do more than just care about being inclusive. You actually have to do something. Being inclusive means taking action. There are so many ways to be inclusive—the possibilities are limitless! Thank the person at the grocery store who spends all day stocking the shelves, learn how to say "Hi!" in Spanish, or start a conversation with the person no one else is talking to.

It's easy to move through life like a robot, just doing our own thing and not worrying about others. We're all so busy, and the easier path is not the inclusive path, but once you become more inclusive, it's like the best french fry you'll ever eat in your life.

One is just never enough.

—The GenderCool Team

About The Authors

Ashton Mota (he/him) is an Afro-Latino college student and advocate for change, driven to achieve justice and equity for all. He was in high school when he wrote this book. A powerful collaborator, Ashton works to create spaces that foster love, acceptance, and partnership.

Rebekah Bruesehoff (she/her) is a high school honors student, influencer, and activist. She was in middle school when she wrote this book. Rebekah inspires people of all ages and identities to show up fully as themselves and dare to make the world a better place.

Their voices help fuel The GenderCool Project, a youth-led movement replacing misinformed opinions with positive experiences meeting transgender and nonbinary youth who are thriving. Through education, advocacy, leadership development, and visibility, GenderCool is uniquely impacting culture, policy, and business worldwide. Learn more at GenderCool.org.

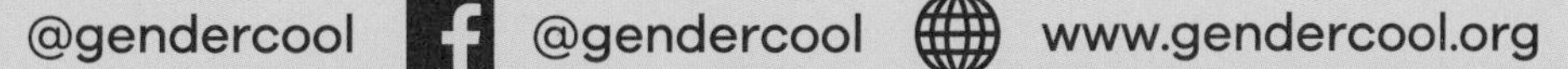

 @gendercool  @gendercool www.gendercool.org